GEORGE GERSHWIN'S

BLUE MONDAY

THE COMPLETE 1922 VOCAL SCORE

George Gershwin, c. 1922

B.G. "Buddy" DeSylva

T0052899

MUSIC BY GEORGE GERSHWIN
TEXT BY B.G. DESYLVA
ADAPTATION BY GEORGE BASSMAN

Cover image of George Gershwin courtesy the Ira and Leonore Gershwin Trusts
Images of B.G. DeSylva (p.1) and scenes from *Rhapsody in Blue* (p.5) courtesy Photofest

Alfred Publishing Co., Inc.
16320 Roscoe Blvd., Suite 100
P.O. Box 10003
Van Nuys, CA 91410-0003
alfred.com

ISBN-10: 0-7390-5506-2
ISBN-13: 978-0-7390-5506-9

Contents

George Gershwin's *Blue Monday*

George Gershwin's desire to produce an opera was something that had been ingrained in him since he started listening to music while growing up in the Lower East Side of New York. His father would often play opera records by the stars of the day on the family Victrola, including those by the field's most celebrated tenor, Enrico Caruso. While learning to write music, Gershwin honed his interest in "serious" music by attending many classical and opera performances, keeping a detailed scrapbook of concerts he attended up until he was 19 years old.

When Gershwin began his career as a song plugger for Jerome H. Remick & Company in 1914, he began combining elements of Tin Pan Alley songwriting with his formal studies in classical music. For a musically insatiable young man like Gershwin, the job was ideal, as it exposed him to a variety of burgeoning American musical styles, including ragtime, early jazz, and blues. By 1916, he had published his first song ("When You Want 'Em, You Can't Get 'Em, When You've Got 'Em, You Don't Want 'Em"), which was followed the next year by his first instrumental (the rag "Rialto Ripples").

When he began writing for the musical theater, Gershwin became acquainted with many of New York's stalwart writers for this field, including a young lyricist named B.G. "Buddy" DeSylva (1895–1950). Before joining his later collaborators, lyricist Lew Brown and composer Ray Henderson, DeSylva teamed up with Gershwin on a number of New York shows, beginning with *La-La-Lucille* in 1919 (joined also by co-lyricist Arthur J. Jackson).

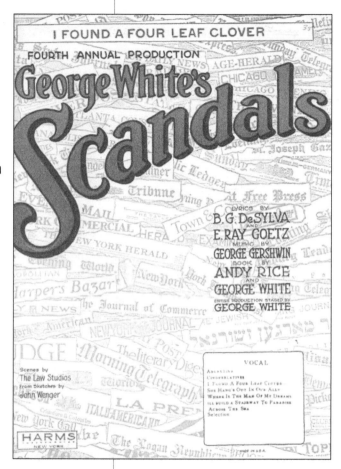

In 1920, Gershwin began writing songs for the *Scandals,* an annual vaudeville revue produced by a former *Ziegfeld Follies* dancer named George White (1892–1968). From 1920 to 1924, Gershwin wrote most of the music for these shows, initially writing with Arthur Jackson, White's in-house lyricist, who was subsequently replaced by DeSylva. For the 1922 edition of *Scandals,* Gershwin and DeSylva came up with the idea of writing an "opera for colored people," which may have been triggered by the success of *Shuffle Along* (1921), an all-black musical written by the team of Eubie Blake and Noble Sissle. DeSylva was aware of Gershwin's budding desire to create concert and stage works and devised a libretto modeled after the African American folksong "Frankie and Albert" (sometimes called "Frankie and Johnny"), which dealt with a jealous woman who shoots her philandering lover because "he done her wrong." George White initially thought that such a piece would not fit in with the lighter fare usually featured in his revue, but, eventually, he reconsidered and about two to three weeks before the show opened, he allowed Gershwin and DeSylva to try out their idea. The work would be later described by Gershwin as a "one-act vaudeville opera," incorporating elements of jazz and blues into a melodramatic skit with a storyline that paralleled plot devices in Italian opera tragedies, most notably, *Pagliacci* by Leoncavallo. Originally titled *Blue Monday Blues*, the work was shortened to *Blue Monday* on Gershwin's short score.

The opera was scored for six black characters (performed by whites in blackface) accompanied by a chorus and the Paul Whiteman orchestra, then the biggest musical draw in the country. White had engaged Whiteman, in addition to other vaudeville stars including W.C. Fields and Ed Wynn, at the handsome rate of two thousand dollars per week. With the prospect of writing for such a prestigious company at hand, Gershwin later recalled that he and DeSylva wrote the entire opera by working steadily for five days and nights. The story was introduced in a recitative prologue, which announced "a colored tragedy enacted in operatic style, and like the white man's opera, the theme will be Love, Hate, Passion and Jealousy!" The ensuing story showed how a jealous and possessive woman's intuition ultimately led to tragedy. Although Gershwin's original condensed score and an orchestration created by William Vodery survived, DeSylva's original text and lyrics were lost (DeSylva would reconstruct it for a revival three years later).

Blue Monday was slated to be performed after the first intermission, encompassing a running time of about 25 minutes. Gershwin would later say that he developed a case of "composer's stomach" before the opera's out-of-town tryout in August 1922. "I can trace my indigestion back to that opening night in New Haven," he recalled later. "My nervousness was mainly due to *Blue Monday*. The show opened and the opera went very well—its only drawback for the show being its tragic ending. I remember one newspaper critic said the following day, in a state of enthusiasm, 'This opera will be imitated in a hundred years.' *Blue Monday* was kept in the show and played one performance in New York [August 28, 1922], the opening night of the show at the Globe Theatre. Mr. White took it out after that, because he said the audience was too depressed by the tragic ending to get into the mood for the lighter stuff that followed."

The opera's prominent placement to lead off Act II could also have caused the work to backfire, especially since the musical number directly preceding the intermission was a performance of Gershwin's jazzy smash hit "I'll Build a Stairway to Paradise," with lyrics by DeSylva and Ira Gershwin (using the pseudonym Arthur Francis). The song was sung by vaudeville sensation Winnie Lightner and featured 50 chorus girls ascending twin circular shimmering white staircases to "heaven," in a kind of visual preamble to the Art Deco spectacles championed by M-G-M film director Busby Berkeley in the 1930s. "Stairway to Paradise" became a huge hit, elevating both George and Ira Gershwin's status as top-flight songwriters. After that opulent and electrifying sequence, it is no wonder that the relatively somber, hastily written opera would be viewed as anticlimactic.

Reaction to *Blue Monday* was mixed, and it is regrettable that it was not given the chance to reverberate in the theatrical world for longer than one performance. Most chose to critique the storyline itself rather than examining the revolutionary musical elements Gershwin was bringing into the theater, although this myopia was repeated when *Porgy and Bess* garnered similar reaction 13 years later.

Although *Blue Monday* disappeared quickly, it made an impression on not only Paul Whiteman, but also Whiteman's arranger and orchestrator, Ferde Grofé, who would later call it a "highly original" work, "representing a new departure in American music." Three years after *Blue Monday*'s demise, Whiteman had Grofé rearrange the work for jazz orchestra, changing its title to *135th Street* and subtitling it a "one-act jazz opera." It was presented as part of Whiteman's *Second Experiment in Modern American Music* at Carnegie Hall on December 29, 1925, and again on January 1, 1926. The concert at Carnegie was publicized as a sequel to the landmark premiere of Grofé's jazz orchestration of *Rhapsody in Blue* at Aeolian Hall on February 12, 1924. Other works featured along with *135th Street* included Grofé's *Mississippi Suite, Circus Day* by Deems Taylor, and John Alden Carpenter's *A Little Piece of Jazz*, among others. Although this lineup was better suited to Gershwin's work than that of a vaudeville revue, it again failed to impress critics, who remained almost universally unenthusiastic about it. When the Whiteman orchestra embarked on a three-month cross-country tour on January 2, *135th Street* had been removed from the program, never to return.

The next appearance of *Blue Monday* came with the release of *Rhapsody in Blue*, a 1945 Hollywood film biography of Gershwin's life starring Robert Alda as the late composer. The opera was used as a plot device to show that Gershwin was ahead of his time with this unique but failed work. For this segment of the film, parts of the original *Blue Monday* storyline were bowdlerized to remove language that might be deemed offensive to film audiences. This pattern continued in the opera's next incarnation, when, on March 29, 1953, Gershwin's opera, still utilizing the title *135th Street,* was presented as part of the *Omnibus* series on CBS television. For this broadcast, a new orchestration was created by George Bassman, which is the basis for this published edition by Alfred. Bassman (1914–1997) had worked previously on Gershwin works, creating orchestrations for the 1937 Hollywood film musical *A Damsel in Distress*.

Re-created scenes from *Blue Monday*, as featured in the 1945 Warner Brothers film, *Rhapsody in Blue*.

Blue Monday marked George Gershwin's first attempt to write in an extended form beyond the restrictions placed upon him by working in musical theater and Tin Pan Alley. Utilizing the looser parameters of long form works, Gershwin was able to establish and recapitulate musical motifs, associate musical elements with characterizations, work with counterpoint, and also experiment for the first time with operatic conventions such as recitative, dance, movement, and pacing. Into this framework, Gershwin folded in blues licks, components of ragtime, and syncopated jazz rhythms and harmonies (especially in the musical interludes), elements that would emerge fully developed in his *Rhapsody in Blue* in 1924. The overall concept and thematic setting of *Blue Monday* also pointed forward to Gershwin's 1935 groundbreaking American opera, *Porgy and Bess.* This extraordinary work shows that, at the early age of 23, the seeds of George Gershwin's genius had not only been planted, but were already germinating.

Cary Ginell
Popular Music Editor
Alfred Publishing Co., Inc.

Blue Monday

Text by B.G. De SYLVA

Music by GEORGE GERSHWIN
Adaptation by GEORGE BASSMAN

PROLOGUE (Sung before curtain)

5 **JOE Poco meno mosso**

La- dies and gen -tle - men!___ Come with me to Mike's col-ored sa-loon and there_ you will see a col-ored trag - e - dy en - act -ed in op- er- at - ic style; and like the white man's op- er- a, the theme will be

love!

Hate!

Pas-sion! Jeal-ous-y.

In this lit - tle plot, you may per-ceive a mor - al,

15 **Maestoso** Enter **TOM**

TOM: *Get out of my way!*

MIKE

Why don't you leave sweet-pea a-lone?

TOM *(ad lib.)*

Keep qui-et! If it was-n't for my sing-ing, you'd have to close this joint.

17 VI Enters

MIKE

Good eve-ning, Vi.

18 VI

Has one of you___ seen___ Joe?___

V. My lov-in' man,_ my_ Joe_____

19 MIKE
I have-n't seen Joe, but if you'll wait a min-ute, I will look in the

M. back room and ask the boys if they have seen him an - y -

he exits   TOM goes to VI

M. where._____

20 TOM *with a beat*

You sure look sweet to-nite, hon-ey. I ain't nev-er seen you look so

T.

fine! **VI** *freely*

I al-ways tries to look my sweet-est when I'm goin' to see my lov-in' joe.

TOM

What do you see in that gam-bler an-y-way? Don't you know that

rit.

a tempo **VI** *Angry and scornful*

T.

I love you? You love me? Who are you?

a tempo *accell.*

V. My Joe may be a gam-bling man, but he's a man.

V. There is no-bod-y like Joe, not in all of the world.

TOM persuasively
Come on, for -

T. get a-bout Joe__ and think a-bout me, Vi. Dont be al-ways cold and

He tries to kiss her

They struggle. **VI** pulls out revolver

T.

dis - tant.____

23 **VI** (*ad lib.*)

My Joe gave me this to use on guys like you.

8va

(8va)

loco

(**MIKE** enters.)

SAM   enter **SAM**

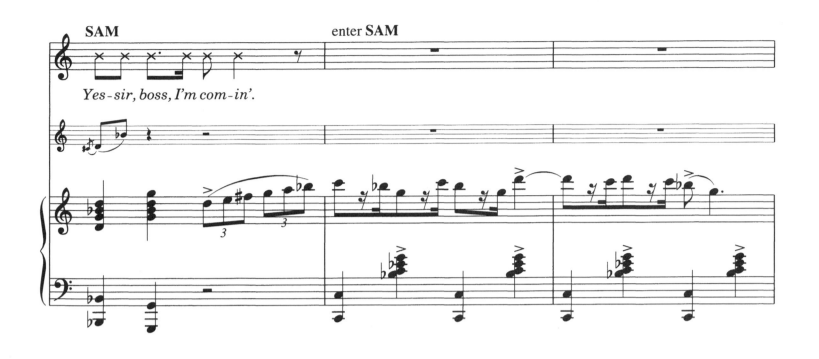

Yes-sir, boss, I'm com-in'.

MIKE

Well, get a move on, you la-zy good-for-noth-in'.

SAM (sweeps floor)

Yes sir, yes sir, boss,

26 SAM

Mon-day's the day_ that all the earth-quakes quiv-er; Mon-day's the day_ they al-ways

(Piano - clars) *(etc.)*

Celesta *8va*

drag the riv - er. Mon-day's a day_ full of sad, sad

news_____ of ships and crews! That's when a gal *gliss.*

will pull a trig - ger; *gliss.* a gal will pull a trig - ger.

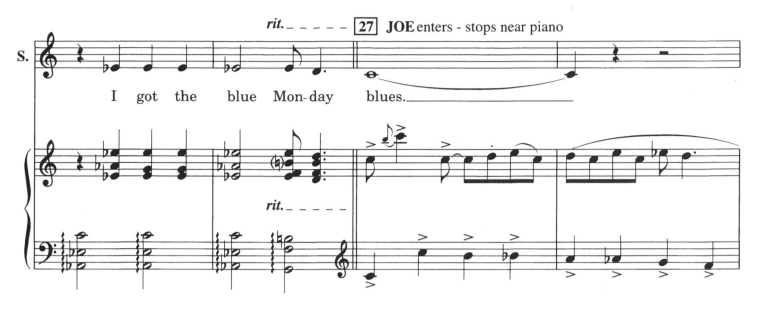

rit. _ _ _ _ _ 　27　 **JOE** enters - stops near piano

S.

I got the blue Mon-day blues._____

TOM sits in back of piano, eavesdrops

JOE

I'll go to her in a

MIKE

Vi was just here look-ing for you; she went up-stairs.

mo-ment; I've got some-thing to tell her.

MIKE

I hear you cleaned up in a

I'll tell the world I did and this is what I'm goin' to do with the

crap game last night.

dough that I won. I'm go-in' South in the morn-in',____

JOE *(ad lib.)*

Vi is so jeal-ous, she'd nev-er let me go for an-y rea-son at all.

32

And

33 *dolce*

I want to see my moth-er, moth-er mine! Oh, how I've missed my

34

moth-er, moth-er mine. May-be I'm a sen-ti-men-tal

Pedal -

32

J. dream- er, but my wea-ry heart will cease to pine

J. when in her arms I whis - per: "I am home a- gain, moth- er mine."

35

MIKE
They shake hands 36

Good luck, Joe.

rit.

So long, Mike. See you lat-er.

I   love but   you, __   my Joe, _____   my Joe. _____

V. I don't want a thing — dear, but you—

V. — But af - ter all, I'm on - ly

hu - man, and I'm a might-y jeal-ous wo - man,

hon - ey. Still, just as long___ as you're true,___

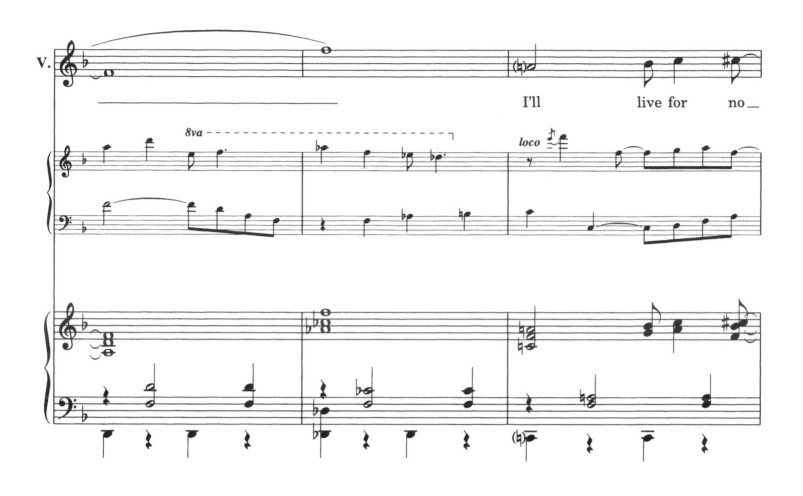

I'll live for no __

__ one but you.

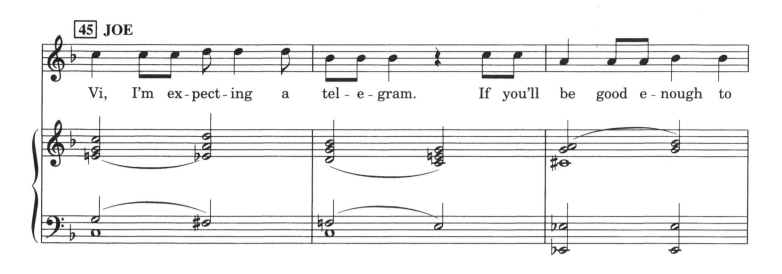

Vi, I'm ex-pect-ing a tel-e-gram. If you'll be good e-nough to

wait, I will see if it has come. _Ex-cuse me._

(JOE exits)

All right, ba-by, but hur-ry back.

(TOM goes to VI's table)
ORCH.

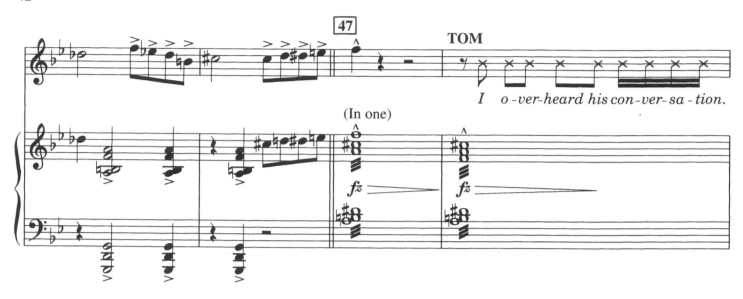

TOM

I o-ver-heard his con-ver-sa-tion.

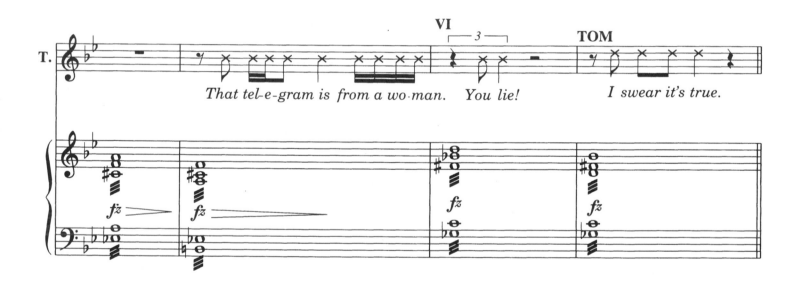

That tel-e-gram is from a wo-man. *You lie!*

I swear it's true.

48 **VI** looks at **TOM** for a moment, turns away, finishes drink in one gulp, stares ahead sullenly.

ORCH.

(In four)

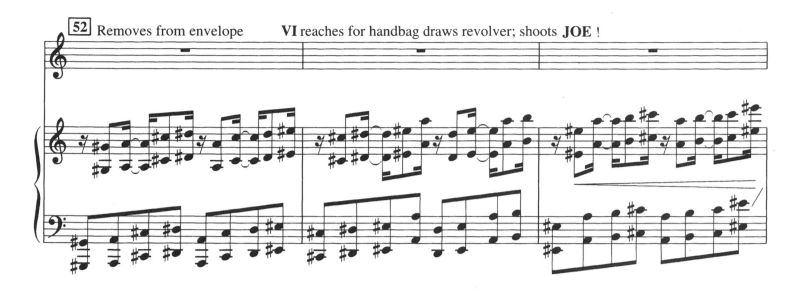

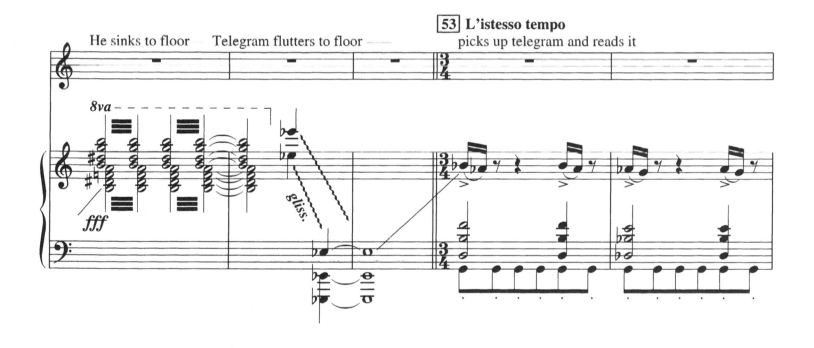

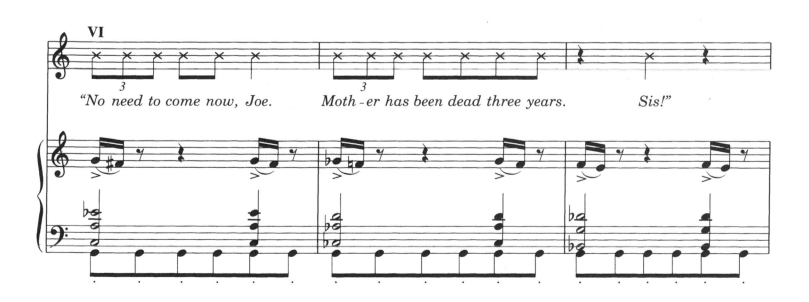

A look of horrible realization comes into
her face; with a moan, she sinks to the floor.

V. Oh, for-

54 JOE

give me. I for - give you.

55

56 Grandioso

J. I'm goin' to see my moth - er, moth - er mine!